DATE DUE			

little whale

little whale

by Ann McGovern

illustrations by John Hamberger

FOUR WINDS PRESS   NEW YORK

LIBRARY OF CONGRESS CATALOGING IN PUBLICATION DATA

McGovern, Ann.
  Little whale.

  SUMMARY: Describes the characteristics and behavior of the whales that
have a small humplike fin on their backs.
  1. Humpback whale — Juvenile literature.
[1. Humpback whale. 2. Whales] I. Hamberger, John. II. Title.
QL737.C424M32   599'.51   78-31737
ISBN 0-590-07630-2

PUBLISHED BY FOUR WINDS PRESS
A DIVISION OF SCHOLASTIC MAGAZINES, INC., NEW YORK, N.Y.
TEXT COPYRIGHT © 1979 BY ANN MCGOVERN
ILLUSTRATIONS COPYRIGHT © 1979 BY JOHN HAMBERGER
ALL RIGHTS RESERVED
PRINTED IN THE UNITED STATES OF AMERICA
LIBRARY OF CONGRESS CATALOG CARD NUMBER: 78-31737

1   2   3   4   5   83   82   81   80   79

To Charles and Eden, *who care about whales
and stars and all things in between.*

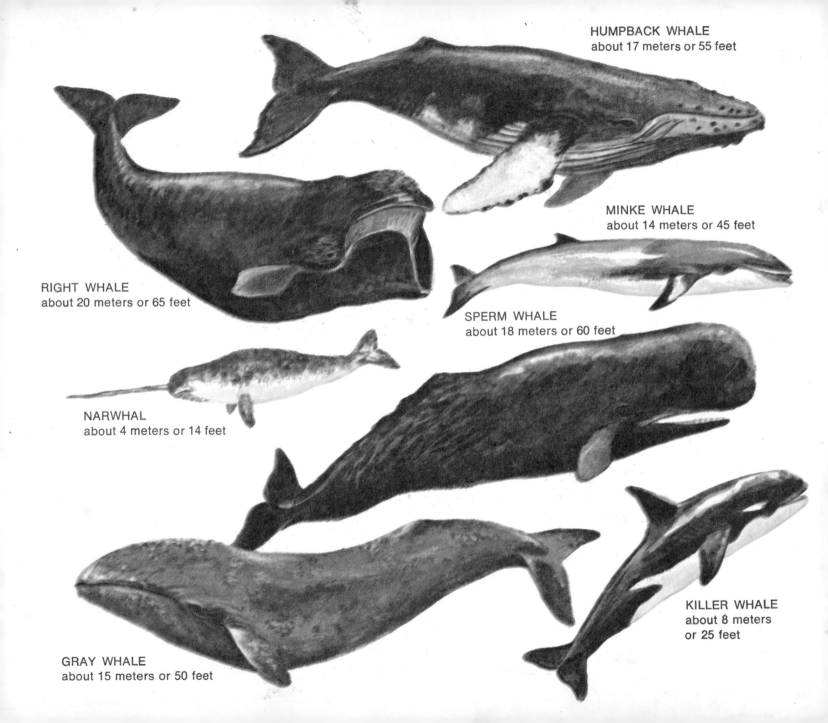

HUMPBACK WHALE
about 17 meters or 55 feet

MINKE WHALE
about 14 meters or 45 feet

RIGHT WHALE
about 20 meters or 65 feet

SPERM WHALE
about 18 meters or 60 feet

NARWHAL
about 4 meters or 14 feet

KILLER WHALE
about 8 meters
or 25 feet

GRAY WHALE
about 15 meters or 50 feet

There are about 80 different kinds of whales
in the oceans of the world.
Small whales. Bigger whales.
And the biggest animals in the world—
the great whales.

This book is about a humpback whale.
The humpback whale is one of the great whales.
It has huge flippers.
It has many little bumps on its body.
The humpback does not have a hump like a camel.
It gets its name from a small fin on its back
that looks a little like a hump.

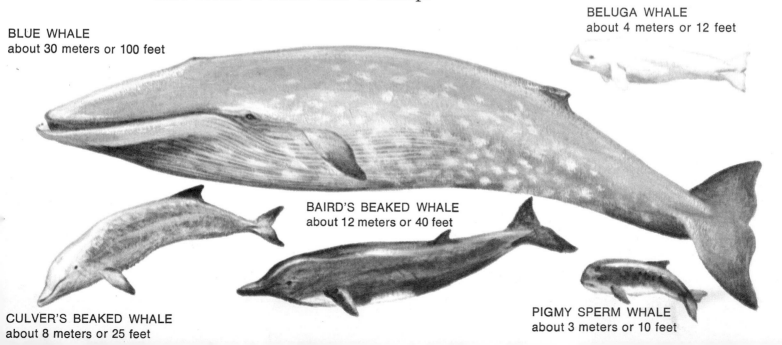

BELUGA WHALE
about 4 meters or 12 feet

BLUE WHALE
about 30 meters or 100 feet

BAIRD'S BEAKED WHALE
about 12 meters or 40 feet

CULVER'S BEAKED WHALE
about 8 meters or 25 feet

PIGMY SPERM WHALE
about 3 meters or 10 feet

Little whale stays close to her mother.
She is only one day old,
but already she weighs a ton.
When she grows up, she will be
almost as long as a city bus.

Little whale was born in the water.
As soon as she was born, she could swim.
She will live in the water all her life.
But she is not a fish.
Whales are mammals and they must breathe air.

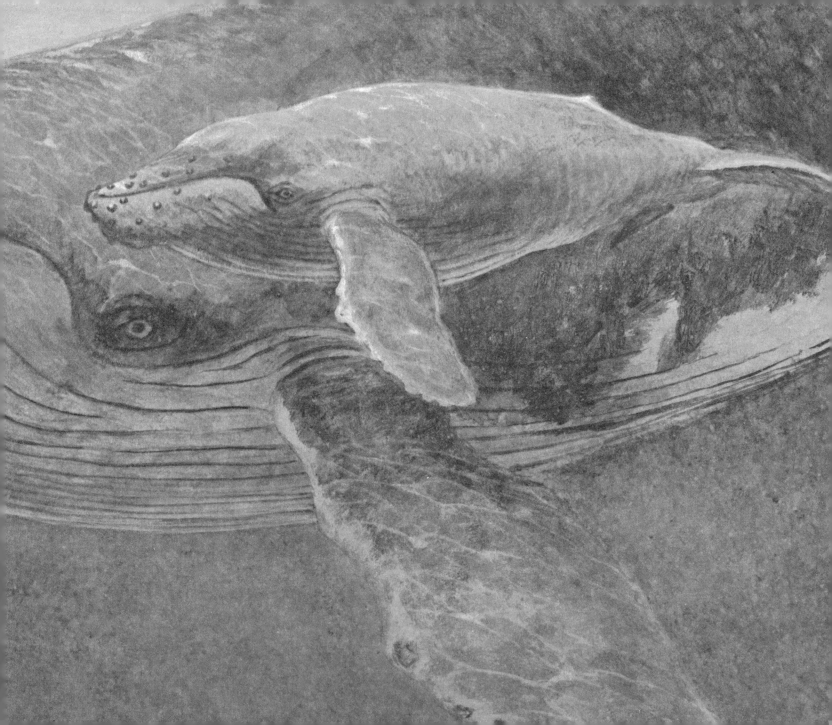

Little whale must come up for air
every few minutes.
When she is older, little whale will be able
to stay underwater about 15 minutes —
sometimes even longer.

When little whale breathes,
a misty fountain of tiny drops of water
shoots into the air.
This fountain is called a *spout*.
A whale breathes through nostrils called
blowholes at the top of its head.

Little whale is hungry.
She drinks the rich milk from her mother's body.
For about a year she will get all the food she needs
from her mother's milk.
Then she will find her own food in the sea.

Mother whale protects her baby
from dangerous sharks.

She teaches her baby everything a
little whale must learn:
    deep-diving
    breath-holding
    leaping clear out of the water
    staying underwater without moving

Little whale practices.
She is learning how to take care of herself.
She is growing bigger.
She no longer has to stay
so close to her mother.

But one day little whale swims too far away.
Father whale sings a low song underwater.
Little whale hears him.
She swims back to the sound of his song.

The sea is full of the songs of humpback whales.
Their songs are whistles and clicks and gurgles,
squeaks and sighs and moans and groans.
Some scientists say that only male whales sing.
They guess it is the way whales keep track of
each other and find each other in the dark sea.

Father whale's song travels far underwater.
It can be heard 160 kilometers* away.

Other humpback whales hear him.
They sing in return.

*100 miles

Dolphins hear him too.
Dolphins are smaller relatives of the
great whales.
The dolphins are playing alongside a ship.
They leap high out of the water
and fall back into the waves.

A pack of hungry killer whales
hears the song of the humpback whale.
The killer whales turn and race toward the sound.

Little whale's mother and father
move closer together.
They put their baby between them.
A hungry killer whale might attack a little whale,
or even a big whale swimming by itself.

One sunny day little whale feels playful.
She does one flip after another.
Up she comes, way out of the water.
She turns in mid-air and lands on her back.

Humpback whales are the most playful of the
great whales.
They are called the acrobats of the sea.
They can leap higher than any other whale.

When whales leap high and fall back — whack —
they may not always be playing.
They may be scratching themselves!
Tiny animals called *barnacles* attach themselves
to whales and grow hard shells.
Scientists think barnacles make whales itch.

One day little whale hears a bubbly sound.
She senses a strange creature nearby.
Like all whales, little whale is curious.
Now she is close enough to see the creature.
It does not look like anything she has seen before.
Not like a fish. Not like a boat.

The scuba diver comes close.
The diver is not afraid.
Whales are big, but they are gentle.

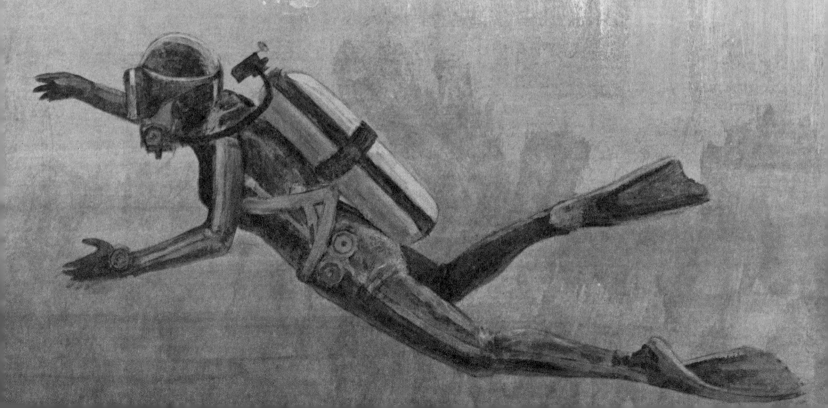

Little whale is growing bigger.
Now she is big enough and strong enough
to make a long journey.
Every year, at the end of winter, the whales
leave the warm tropical waters.
There is not enough food for adult whales here.
They must travel to where the waters are cold
and filled with good things for whales to eat.

Father whale sings a song underwater.
His song may mean, "Time to go."

Now the whales gather for the journey.
They will travel together in groups.
A group of whales is called a *pod*.
A pod may have as few as three whales
or as many as fifteen.

A whale's journey is called a *migration*.
The journey may be thousands of kilometers long.
It may take three months.

Day and night,
the whales move slowly through the water.
They hardly rest.

How do whales find their way
across the wide, wide ocean?
Maybe the sun guides them by day.
Maybe the stars guide them by night.
Maybe the older whales remember
some of the things they passed on other journeys.
A wreck of a ship. Or an underwater mountain.

No one knows for sure how whales find their way.
But year after year whales return to the same place.

Now the whales have reached the cold waters.
The long journey is over.
The whales will stay in these waters for many months.

Little whale does not feel cold.
Whales have layers of fat called *blubber*.
Blubber helps to keep them warm.

Now there is plenty of food to eat.
Humpback whales eat little fish
and small shrimp called *krill*.
The big whales can gulp a million krill
in one mouthful!

One day, little whale watches a big humpback whale
make a net of bubbles to catch fish.
The whale swims below a school of fish.
Then it blows bubbles in the water.
As the whale swims up, its bubbles form a column.
Many fish are trapped in this column of bubbles!

Humpback whales don't have teeth.
They have a kind of strainer called *baleen*.
A humpback whale takes in a big mouthful of sea water
filled with tiny creatures.
Then the whale closes its huge jaws.
It raises its tongue and forces the water out.
But the tiny creatures do not escape.
They are held back by the bristly baleen
to make a good meal for the whale.

Now the days are getting frosty with cold.
There are many icebergs.
Only a few animals can live in such cold.
Little whale sees walruses and seals,
and big birds called puffins.

One day a big ship steams into the cold waters.
It is a whale-hunting ship.
A helicopter flies above the ship,
tracking down whales.

Little whale hears the boom of a deadly weapon,
exploding and killing a big humpback whale.

The men haul the dead whale up to their ship.
They cut the whale to pieces.
They freeze the whale meat
and boil the bones and fat to make oil.

Little whale and her family are lucky.
They have escaped from the whale killers.

Every day the ice gets thicker.
The icebergs look like mountains of ice above the water.
And they are even bigger underneath.

The whales must start their long journey back
to the warm waters.
They must leave soon
before they are trapped by the ice.

Five years pass.
Five years of long journeys
from warm to cold waters and back again.
Now little whale is grown up.

One day she hears a whale singing a special
song in the sea.
Little whale swims to him.
They will swim close together.
They will mate.
And next year she will have
a little whale of her own.

A NOTE FROM THE AUTHOR:

Maybe this story will have a happy ending.
And maybe it won't.

Every year too many great whales are killed.
They are killed mostly for their blubber
which is made into oil.
Whale oil is used to make soap and shoe polish,
lipstick and paint.

The truth is that all these things don't have
to be made from whale oil.
They could be made from other kinds of oil.

People who care about whales are trying
to find new ways to stop the killing
of thousands of whales.

If the killing goes on, whales may become *extinct*.
Extinct means there are no more.
Extinct means there never will be any more.
No more little whales in the sea.
No more whales calling their songs
through the wide, wide waters.

Whale Words

BALEEN: Humpback whales and other baleen whales strain their food through the bristly baleen in their mouths. Any whale that doesn't have teeth is called a baleen whale.

BLOWHOLES: Whales' nostrils are called blowholes. Baleen whales have two nostrils in the top of their head.

BLUBBER: Blubber is a thick layer of fat underneath the whale's skin. Blubber helps keep whales warm.

BREACHING: Breaching is leaping clear up out of the water.

BULL: A bull is a male whale.

CALF: A calf is a young whale.

CETACEAN: Scientific word to describe all whales, dolphins, and porpoises in the world.

COW: A cow is a female whale.

FLIPPERS: Flippers stick out from each side of the whale. They are used for balancing and steering through the water. The humpback whale has the longest flippers of all the whales—one-third as long as its body.

FLUKES: The two halves of a whale's tail are called flukes. They are flat and stick out sideways. Whales swim by moving their powerful flukes up and down.

KRILL: Large numbers of small shrimp, called krill, are eaten by baleen whales.

MIGRATION: A whale's long journey is called a migration. Humpback whales migrate every summer to cold waters to feed and swim back to warm waters in winter. They may travel thousands of kilometers.

POD: A group of whales is called a pod. There may be from three to fifteen whales in a pod.

SOUNDING: Sounding is another name for deep-diving. Whales can't stay underwater for a very long time. They must come up to breathe.

SPOUTING: A whale breathes out the warm air in its lungs through its blowholes to form a misty fountain. This is called spouting.

THAR SHE BLOWS: In the old whale-hunting days, when a whaler spotted a spouting whale, he called out "Thar she blows!" Whalers could tell from a distance what kind of whale it was from the shape of the spout.